Golden Era
The Heart of Wisconsin Sidelines

Kris Leonhardt • Tori Wittenbrock

Golden Era
The Heart of Wisconsin Sidelines

Kris Leonhardt • Tori Wittenbrock

Copyright © Multi Media Channels, 2025

All rights reserved.

Except for brief quotations in news articles or reviews, no part of this book may be reproduced in any manner without prior written permission of the publisher: teachingpress@uwgb.edu

Some passages in this book were previously published in Press Times print and digital editions.

ISBN: 979-8-9938316-0-2

Printed, bound, and distributed by IngramSpark

Cover and interior design by Alex Kunce

Illustrations by Jordan Sieracki

Mimi & Rupert Books

is an imprint of The Teaching Press at UW-Green Bay

A student-powered, community-serving publisher and printer in Northeastern Wisconsin

University of Wisconsin-Green Bay

2420 Nicolet Drive, Green Bay, Wisconsin 54311-7001

✉ teachingpress@uwgb.edu   @theteachingpress   blog.uwgb.edu/teaching-press

The Green Bay Packers emerged from the frozen heartland in 1919, a scrappy collection of local heroes who dared to challenge the football establishment when professional leagues were still finding their footing. From humble beginnings, the Packers forged a legacy that would outlast others and prove that greatness knows no zip code. By the team's side were a grateful public and a band of merry musicians, the Lumberjack Band, and later a group of cheerleaders, the Golden Girls.

This book is dedicated to those performers who braved the cold Wisconsin football weather to entertain the crowds and support the legendary team.

Table of Contents

Table of Contents . . . vii

Foreword ix

The Lumberjack Band

A Lesson in Spirit. 13

Dusting Off the Red Flannel 15

Hayseeds Don't March 16

Return of the Razzle-Dazzle 17

"Go! You Packers Go!" 18

The Leader of the Band 20

The Make-Up of the Band 22

The Majorettes 24

Sidelined 25

Mary Jane

An Early Start 30

A Rising Star 32

The Golden Era 34

Everyone's a Star 35

Passing the Baton. 36

The Show Goes On. 40

A Great Love Story. 42

A Lasting Impression 44

The Golden Girls

The Women on the Sidelines 48

The First to Do It. 56

A Lasting Experience 58

An Evolving Presence. 60

Once in a Lifetime 64

Acknowledgements 69

Photo Credits 72

Foreword

Kris Leonhardt's last book about Curly Lambeau [*Lambeau: The Boy Behind Green Bay Football*] was a winner. It helped Packers fans understand his inception and the continuation of the Green Bay Packers team, as well as the iconic history that endures today.

Kris Leonhardt and Tori Wittenbrock then had another concept in publicizing the history of the Packers, to show Packers fans — young and old — what makes the Packers great.

This book is not about Packers players, Packers coaches, or even Packers fans; it is about the entertainment during Packers games that made the fans and athletes smile — the Packers Lumberjack Band and the Golden Girls.

In this book, you will learn how the Lumberjack Band was started.

Not only did they play at local Green Bay games, but they also traveled to other cities where the Packers were playing.

The information on how this band's name and clothing was changed is an interesting story, stemming from Vince Lombardi's "recommendation."

The Golden Girls started with Mary Jane Van Duyse-Sorgel showing her abilities to spin her baton and dance for many years. She had already made the Packers and Packers fans smile, not only in Green Bay but in other football venues.

Again, Vince Lombardi had a good idea to have a group of cheerleaders for the Packers. Mary Jane became the head of the Golden Girls and created entertainment that thrilled the crowds.

This book is an excellent way to gain an understanding of the Green Bay Packers' rich and exciting history.

Enjoy and learn,

Donald R. Sipes II, M.D.

Packers Hall of Fame Inc. President

The Lumberjack Band

by Kris Leonhardt

A Lesson in Spirit

Acme Packing Company's Emmett Clair and Curly Lambeau returned from Chicago on November 25, 1921, after attending the Staley-Buffalo game on Thanksgiving Day.

Lambeau's message to the public via the Press-Gazette stated: "We'll beat them. After giving the Staleys the once-over, I feel confident that the Packers will be champions of the Middle West Sunday night. Come on down, fans, and let's show Chicago that Green Bay is the best little football town in the country."

The Packers stood in fourth place in the American Professional Football League, trailing behind the Buffalo, the Decatur Staleys, and Akron. That Sunday's game against the Staleys at Chicago's Cub Park would prove crucial, as their records were close and a win would place the Packers in a position to obtain the championship.

"When the Green Bay Packers go to Chicago after the professional football title, they will be accompanied by a bigger delegation of rooters than accompanied them to the Cardinals game last Sunday and by a rooters band of 20 pieces. An appeal was sent out to fans to make it possible for the band to accompany the team, by making contributions," another Press-Gazette piece stated.

"On Saturday night, band members gathered at DeLair's Café and marched with their instruments in tow to the North Western depot, where a large crowd awaited them. Upon boarding the train, the band members gathered in an empty baggage car and held a rehearsal until the wee hours," wrote Cliff Christl in The Greatest Story in Sports.

"Upon arriving in Chicago in the early dawn, band members and fans — two abreast and a block long — merrily marched through The Loop. It was the makeshift beginning of what became the Packers' famous Lumberjack Band.

"Dressed in corduroy pants, woolen shirts, mackinaws, hunting caps, and high boots, they stopped to perform in several hotel lobbies and were reprimanded by police for not having a parade permit before arriving at the Stratford, the Packers' hotel.

"The manager of the Morrison Hotel, which had been one

The Lumberjack Band poses with their musical instruments in 1923. The band members are wearing coats, hats, and flannel shirts.

of their stops, broke open several boxes of cigars for his seemingly harmless assailants. But later, at the Stratford, restaurateur George DeLair, who organized the band, broke the diamond-studded leg off the piano stool in the Grand Ballroom and used it as a baton. From there, the band headed to Cubs Park, where members created another scene, yelling battle cries and playing their favorite tunes, 'On Wisconsin' and 'How Dry I Am.'"

"Reaching the field early, they stepped out along the

A 1929 ad invites fans to travel with the Lumberjack Band.

gridiron, and the band killed the dreary moments before the team got on the field. George DeLair, Harry Annen, Jock Smith, and Sheriff Nick Ryan were in the limelight, and they cut up all sorts of capers to the music of the band," the Press-Gazette later recapped.

"Throughout the game, even when things weren't breaking for Green Bay, the Badger rooters kept up their yelling, and no better support has ever been seen here, even at a college game."

Although the fans witnessed a devastating 20-0 loss against the Staleys, the Decatur, Illinois, team got a lesson in spirit, as the band held court until the last car pulled out of the train station on Monday morning.

"Never in my experience have I ever witnessed a better display of spirit. I have often been told that Green Bay was one of the best sporting towns in the Northwest. I believe it now, and one thing is sure: hereafter, whenever a Green Bay team comes to Chicago, they will be given a warm welcome," expressed Ed Smith, dean of the Chicago Sport Writers.

Dusting Off the Red Flannel

"The Lumberjack Band is assured. Tony Vandenberg and Ernie Stiller are rounding up the musicians. The band will be 20 strong and every member will be 'togged out' in the Lumberjack togs like they used when they 'burned' up Chicago two years ago," a November 15, 1923, Press-Gazette stated.

"The bandsmen are donating their services. They will make the trip in a big truck owned by the Leight Transfer Co. This company is only charging for the driver's salary and the oil and gas en route. Meals for the band total $30. Each of the musicians will be allowed two meals at 75 cents apiece. The total cost of the trip will be under $70, and this money has been raised by 'dollar' volunteers."

The list of those donating to deploy the Lumberjack Band was printed the following day — a list that included G.W. Calhoun, A.B. Turnbull, George Abrams, and about 70 other supporters.

"Hundreds of Bayites will invade Milwaukee for the Sabbath day tilt," the paper stated. "Eight hundred seats located in the west stands, directly in the center of the field, have been saved for Green Bay's followers. Special seats have been set up for the famous Lumberjack Band and the funmakers."

The Lumberjack Band dusted off their sheepskin and red flannel and began practice.

"Every member of the band is a crackerjack musician, and they have had several rehearsals in order to put their stuff over with a bang," the paper added. "A set of Packer yells has been drawn up and printed. They will be handed out to the Green Bay spectators..."

The press leading up to the game must have done its job, for when Sunday rolled around, it was estimated that the Green Bay supporters totaled a thousand, cheering the team on to a 10-7 win.

"The Lumberjack Band more than lived up to advance notices. When they came out of the dugout, a roar of applause made them welcome. The Bay Band marched around the field, cutting loose with popular tunes, and when they got back to the home plate, they played 'On Wisconsin' while the entire assemblage rose to their feet. The band tooted their horns all during the game while the leaders cut all sorts of fancy capers. Bryan 'Mulligan' Seroogy amused the crowd with his fancy steps," the Press-Gazette game coverage stated.

An early photo of the Lumberjack Band performing.

Hayseeds Don't March

It was November 1927 before the community came together again for a "fund gathering" to get the Lumberjack Band transported back to Chicago for the final game of that season.

Contribution buckets were circulated around City Stadium during the Dayton-Packers game the week before the Packers-Chicago clash.

"The members of the American Legion Band, who will turn Lumberjacks for a period of about 35 hours, are getting together their hob-nailed shoes, rough mackinaws, and corduroy pants for the occasion. On about next Tuesday, the musicians will start letting their whiskers grow to complete the lumberjack picture," a Nov. 9 Press-Gazette article stated.

The Lumberjack Band accompanied the Packers, along with an estimated 1,000 fans, to help cheer the team to a 14-6 win over the Bears.

The following year, the band traveled to Wrigley Field once again for the Packers' October match with the Bears, and walked away with a reported world record.

"The Green Bay American Legion band — the lumberjack organization that played for the Packers-Bears game in Chicago on Sunday — claims a world record for continuous playing without stopping to change music, or for any other reason," an October 23, 1928, Press-Gazette story stated.

"The bandsmen dressed as lumberjacks, marched in ragged formation, and were purposely out of step, a fact that may not have been appreciated by the WGN radio announcer, the band thinks, but surely was appreciated by both the Green Bay and Chicago fans."

The following week, the band was back on the field as the Packers beat Dayton 17-0 at City Stadium. Whether at home or taking the train to Chicago, the band made a big show of it, marching from the Elks Club to the Northwestern train, forming a parade in their Lumberjack gear.

In 1929, 1930, and 1931, the band continued to return to the Chicago games to cheer on the Packers, financed by a community collection; however, area residents began to struggle with their non-conventional attire. While locals voiced their displeasure, a Green Bay resident defended their choice.

"Our band tries to be something really different, not to the point of having hay in their hair, but rather as something novel and unique. They do not make Chicago fans think of us as a bunch of hicks, because 'hayseeds' do not march or play like our band does. Appearance counts a lot, so it is used in this case for effect," a "Packers and Band Booster" wrote in the October 13, 1931, Press-Gazette.

Return of the Razzle-Dazzle

For many years, the Lumberjack Band was formed from members of the American Legion Band. However, a disagreement between the American Legion and the band occurred in the years following 1929, and the band subsequently severed ties with the organization.

On June 6, 1933, the American Legion Band was no more, after the Green Bay City Council adopted a resolution to designate it the "Green Bay City Band."

Five days later, the group made their first appearance as the Green Bay City Band. Little mention of the Lumberjack Band is made during the following years, and the razzle-dazzle was limited to the action on the playing field.

In the fall of 1939, with the team aiming for its fifth national title, plans were being made for the Lumberjack Band's triumphant return for a Sunday Packers-Chicago Cardinals game, with the musicians starting their training at the same time as the team's players.

"When the Packer corporation decided to seek the formation of a band, largely as a showmanship project to add to the color at games, the services of men qualified by experience and reputation in the musical field were sought.

The result was pretty much the same as when Coach Curly Lambeau recruited his gridders — an all-star organization with a specialist at every post in the lineup," Dick Flatley wrote in the September 13, 1939, Press-Gazette.

"Alex V. Enna, veteran instructor and conductor, was named director. Wilmer Burke was made business manager. Together, they laid plans for such a band as the Packer officials seemed to desire.

"All the musicians were selected in Green Bay and De Pere. Many of them are comparatively young — products of the school musical systems in the two cities. Others have been prominent in Green Bay musical circles for several years."

Enna said that he was "deeply gratified to the Packers for giving Green Bay and De Pere musicians something to work for."

"Through the efforts of Mr. Lee Joannes, Coach Lambeau, and the other Packer officials, enough interest has been aroused to see a real band through. I believe that this organization will be of real benefit to the community at large as well as the Packers."

"Go! You Packers Go!"

Back in 1931, the Lumberjack Band was leading the crowd with the fight song, "Go! You Packers Go!" — composed and written by Erich Karll.

"The original idea for the Packers song was one of those things which seemed like a 'screwball' idea at the time but which caught on and paid off," a September 4, 1953, Press-Gazette article stated.

"Karll lived in Green Bay at the time and wrote the words for the song. He pestered a number of musicians to help him set it to music."

One day, Karll went to the radio station WHBY, where local musician Billy Burt sat down at the piano and created the sheet music.

"And then, in 1930, Karll had the song copyrighted and published," the article added.

In September 1939, Sports Editor John Walter from the Press-Gazette wrote that the song was being revived for the rebirth of the Lumberjack Band.

"Alex Enna is having some New York arrangers work on 'Go! You Packers Go!' to get a more satisfactory arrangement, one which will show to the best advantage of his particular grouping of instruments," he stated.

The new Lumberjack "swing band" made its first appearance dressed in bright, colorful uniforms as they cheered on the Green Bay Packers against the Chicago Cardinals on September 17, 1939.

Tony and Jim Collard were the only original band members who reprised their roles in the reboot of the band according to Walter.

When performing for games, the band was often joined by members of local high school groups.

"We have been sold on the Packers Lumberjack Band ever since it was organized, and Sunday it sounded peppier than ever, established in an attractive shell at the northwest corner of the gridiron. We feel, too, that additional musical organizations add to, rather than subtract from, the utility of the Lumberjack group," Walter wrote in 1940.

"Go! You Packers Go!"

Hail, hail, the gang's all here to yell for you,

Hail, hail, the gang's all here to yell for you,

And keep you going in your winning ways,

Hail, hail, the gang's all here to tell you, too,

That, win or lose, we'll always sing your praises, Packers;

Go, you Packers, go and get 'em

Go, you fighting fools, upset 'em

Smash their line with all your might

A Touchdown, Packers, Fight! Fight! Fight,

Fight on, you Blue and Gold, to glory

Win this game, the same old story,

Fight, you Packers,

Fight, and bring the bacon home to
OLD GREEN BAY.

The Leader of the Band

In 1939, the Lumberjack Band "swing band" was performing at all Green Bay Packers' home games, as well as concert dates at the Columbus Club, featuring 25 musicians.

When the team stepped off the Milwaukee Road train that December, the Lumberjack Band was there, along with hundreds of people crowding Washington Street, from Mason to Chicago, to welcome home the champions.

"Hundreds of fans who turned out yesterday had seen the Green Bay-New York game at Milwaukee with their own eyes," the Press-Gazette stated the following day, "but their numbers made it appear that the team had returned home from a distant battle.

"At the north end of the platform, two Wisconsin Public Service buses, a pumper of fire station number one, and a Leicht truck containing the red-coated Packers Lumberjack Band, were drawn up in parade formation. The band worked hard and effectively on such bits as the Packers' pep song, 'On Wisconsin,' and the new national anthem, 'The Beer Barrel Polka,' set the pace as the small parade moved down the street, followed by a vast and admiring throng."

In 1940, Lumberjack Band Business Manager Wilner Burke was named band director, a title he held until he resigned in the early 1980s.

"Burke first played in the makeshift Lumberjack Band as far back as the early 1930s. The origin of the early 'Jacks', as they were known, dated to 1921, the Packers' first year in what is now the National Football League," wrote Packers Historian Cliff Christl.

"Along with directing the band, Burke could also pitch in and play the saxophone. His duties included arranging the Packers' halftime shows. In 1966, Burke was named chairman of the NFL's halftime directors.

"During his 42-year association with the Packers, Burke

In 1940, Lumberjack Band Business Manager Wilner Burke was also named band director, a title he held until his resignation in the early 1980s.

In this undated photo, Wilner Burke is pictured at the far left standing.

built the Lumberjack Band into a unit which not only became synonymous with the team, but gained its own fame and following through its lively performances at both games and special events."

Burke also served on the Green Bay City Council for over two decades, as well as the Brown County Board of Supervisors. He passed away in 1985 and was inducted posthumously into the Green Bay Packers Hall of Fame in 1986.

"He was a wonderful director, very strong," then band director, Lovell Ives, told Keith Goldschmidt shortly after Burke's death. "He ran the band with a great deal of care. He really put himself into it. I don't think he ever missed a game. He had a lot of pride in the group."

The Make-Up of the Band

"Those intimately concerned with the destinies of the Green Bay Packers have seen for some time that a football game, even a bang-up battle, is not quite enough entertainment for the average fan. The result has been the formation and financial sponsorship of the Green Bay Packers Lumberjack Band," Sports Writer Ray Pagel stated in his column "Looking Up" in 1942.

"Any summary of the band personnel would not be complete without mention of little Carol Jean Collard, the three-year-old daughter of one of the drummers. Carol showed a keen interest in music when she was little more than a year old, and it was not long before she began to beg to be a musician too."

Little Carol had her chance when she was given a uniform and named a drum majorette.

"When Director Wilner Burke saw the enthusiastic response to this addition to the band's usual program of marches and popular numbers, an idea germinated," Lee Remmel wrote in 1948.

Drum Section

Walter Remick, 30 years of experience.
Art Andre, 25 years of experience.
Jimmy Collard, 20 years of experience.

Bass Horn Section

Wendell Shaw, 25 years of experience.
Bob Sheffers, 15 years of experience.

Trombone Section

Donald Barber, 12 years of experience.
Bob LeClaire, 8 years of experience.
James Weizenegger, 6 years of experience.
Clyde Plog IV plays with the Nicolet High School Band.

Brass Section

Herb Hall, 30 years of experience.
Leo Klamert, 27 years of experience.
Elmer Kaap, 15 years of experience.
William Johnson, 15 years of experience.
Merrill Guerin, 12 years of experience.
Quentin Willems, 10 years of experience.
Harold Ecker, 7 years of experience.

Saxophone Section

Joe Hartinger, 15 years of experience.
Ray DuPuis, 15 years of experience.
Norbert Ecker, 10 years of experience.
Gordon Beseau, 10 years of experience.

Clarinet Section

Russ Walters, 15 years of experience.
Howard Sheldon, 15 years of experience.
James Aerts, 10 years of experience.
Don Shultz, 6 years of experience.

Carol Collard (second from left) is pictured with fellow Lumberjack Band majorettes Germaine Pirlot (left) and Gloria Birmingham (right) in 1944.

The Majorettes

Carol Jean Collard wasn't quite three when she started with the Lumberjack Band and is noted as the band's first majorette.

"Within the next several years, the Packers band drum majorette became a permanent fixture at Packers home games, both in Green Bay and in Milwaukee," wrote Lee Remmel.

Each year, tryouts were held for young ladies interested in entertaining with a baton and executing complex formations, with the top three individuals selected to perform with the band in Green Bay.

Three other Milwaukee girls were selected to appear with the band at State Fair Park in West Allis for the Milwaukee games.

The majorettes took lessons from Don Marcouiller, in De Pere, who was a former national high school champion and one-time major of the Lumberjack Band; he later led the University of Wisconsin band.

In the 1940s, the band donned red and green uniforms — trying to keep with the lumberjack theme — and was just one of two bands in professional football at the time.

In 1948, the number of majorettes went from three to six, selected by tryouts.

The band also had one major, including Don Marcouiller in the early years and longtime major Bruce Stengel.

Other early Green Bay majorettes included: Germaine Pirlot, Shirley Schwaller, Marge Lambert, Rosemary Schwebs, Phyllis Kessler, Bernadine Boyere, Beth Gale, Pat Lison, Dolores Vander Loop, LaVona Lefebvre, Sharrell Wadzinski, Jane Sibilsky, Pat Parins, Susie Nelson, Donna Weckler, and Shirley Remich, daughter of band drummer Walter Remich.

In the early 1950s, Mary Jane Van Duyse joined the band as a majorette while teaching dance and twirling at her Sturgeon Bay studio.

"At the urging of Wilner Burke, the leader of the Packer Lumberjack Band, Mary Jane auditioned in 1949 to join the Packerettes of the Packer Lumberjack Band. She was the Packer drum majorette from 1951 to 1966. She was named 'Miss Majorette of America' in 1953 and in 1956," Mary Jane's obituary later recalled.

Van Duyse became head majorette in 1954, replacing Bernadine Boyere, who retired that year. Mary Jane went on to become an enigma in her own right.

In the 1960s, when Vince Lombardi urged her to work on another project, Mary Jane retired as the head majorette, and LeAnn Christiansen took over. According to the Press-Gazette, Christiansen was a protégé of Bruce Stengel, the former drum major.

The original majorette, young Carol Jean Collard, spent 12 years with the band before joining the Dominican Sisters. In 1957, she entered the order at Sinsinawa, based in Hazel Green.

Sidelined

"Before the 1963 season, the Packers' famous Lumberjack Band changed its name to the Green Bay Packer Band, and members abandoned their old outfits for green blazers and gray trousers with gold stripes. Word was Vince Lombardi wanted the band to have a more sophisticated look," Packers Historian Cliff Christl wrote in The Greatest Story in Sports.

By 1969, 120 different musicians had played with the band, and that year's group boasted 11 area band directors.

"At the height of its popularity, the band also played for special Packers events and rallies, and marched in parades, and played for stage shows throughout Wisconsin," Christl said.

Heading up the band through it all was Wilner Burke, who served as director for over four decades until resigning prior to the 1982 season. That summer, the Packers corporation was looking to make some changes.

"The Packers band, upon recommendation of the entertainment committee of the team's board of directors, will play predominantly swing music next season and forego the usual marches that have been the trademark of the band and its predecessor, the Lumberjack Band," Tony Walter wrote in the Press-Gazette.

"It is all part of the Packers corporation's attempt to build upon the atmosphere of fan enthusiasm that highlighted the second half of the 1981 season."

Lovell Ives took over as band director in 1982.

"When Ives took over in 1982, he brought changes to the band, formerly called the Lumberjack Swing Band," Patty Hoeft wrote in the Press-Gazette.

"We went from a military band, playing a lot of marches, to playing more popular music, up-to-date music," Ives, then a UW-Green Bay music professor, told Hoeft.

Ives' iteration of the band included representation from some of the Green Bay area's top bands at the time — River City Six, Street Life, Charisma, The Diplomats, Deans of Dixieland, and Woody & Friends.

"Positioned on the sidelines near the 15-yard line on the southwest corner, Ives calls the plays, matching melodies with football action on the field," Hoeft stated.

"If we're behind 20 points, the band can't play 'Mission Impossible' or 'Wipeout.' It's important that tunes are played at the right time," Ives said.

In 1999, the Packer Band was "sidelined from the sidelines," Susan Campbell wrote in the Press-Gazette.

"The band, a Green Bay Packers institution since 1921, will take its act to the tailgaters outside Lambeau Field for the 2-1/2 hour strolling concert before each game."

By the time they were asked to perform for tailgaters, the band had been formally performing at Packers games for six decades.

The Lumberjack Band on the field at City Stadium in an undated photo.

Mary Jane
Green Bay's Golden Girl

by Kris Leonhardt

An Early Start

"She was a very gregarious person. Everyone knew Mary Jane, and Mary Jane knew everyone else, especially in the Green Bay area," Dave Sorgel said of his stepmother, Mary Jane Van Duyse-Sorgel. "She was the epitome of the Green Bay Packers. If you said Green Bay Packers back in the day, you thought of Mary Jane."

A much younger Mary Jane Van Duyse started her dance career at the Dorothy Leyse La Plant School of Dancing at the age of six.

Three years later, she began twirling a baton and started wowing the crowds at regional festivals with her acrobatics and baton twirling skills while attending Sevastopol School. She later became majorette of the high school band.

Mary Jane's parents, Frances and Gertrude Van Duyse, owned and operated Vans Tavern and resided above the bar. Living in town gave Mary Jane easy access to available facilities where she began training and sharing her skills with others.

Before graduating from Sevastopol High School, she began nurturing her first set of students in tap, ballet, acrobatics, ballroom dance, roller skating, and baton twirling. She hosted her first recital, "Dance Follies of 1951," at the Brussels High School auditorium a month before she graduated. Two months later, she hosted another recital for her students at Sturgeon Bay High School.

In August, Mary Jane won the state championship in baton twirling after being chosen as Miss Majorette of America and being featured in Drum Major magazine.

She garnered another state championship win in 1953 and went on to capture the National Class A Baton Twirling Championship in 1954.

At the age of 17, she was approached by Packers Lumberjack Band Director Wilner Burke, who urged her to audition for the Packerettes, starting a longtime relationship with the organization. Her win in the national championships placed a spotlight on the Packers Lumberjack Band, as she traveled the state performing in school auditoriums and local events.

In January 1955, Mary Jane announced that she was "hanging up her batons."

"Twelve years ago, a baton twirler in Sturgeon Bay said she would quit when she had won a national championship,"

Mary Jane Van Duyse started her dance career at the Dorothy Leyse La Plant School of Dancing at the age of six. Three years later, she began twirling a baton and started wowing the crowds at regional festivals with her acrobatics and baton twirling skills.

a January 28, 1955, Press-Gazette article stated. "That ambition was realized by 21-year-old Mary Jane Van Duyse last August. Today, she is through with competitions and will make only a few personal tours, so she declares.

"Last August at Kenosha, Mary Jane entered the Roundup Open National tournament and, despite heavy competition, walked off with the first prize. A month before, in Milwaukee, she had copped another national championship. These titles are in addition to the two state championships that she has won."

The article stated that Mary Jane's next focus would be on helping her students gain one of the recognitions she had received."

Mary Jane poses for a photo, featuring her stand-out Golden Girl outfit and her baton.

A Rising Star

After announcing her retirement from competition, Mary Jane continued to serve as a majorette for the Green Bay Packers Lumberjack Band. She also continued to teach dance, baton twirling, and other classes, while mentoring young women — something she continued to do throughout her life. Mary Jane's stepson, Dave Sorgel, and his wife, Collette, said that she held those she mentored to a "high standard."

"Basically, she helped everybody. She tried to get women to do their makeup, their hair, dress properly, and always be poised," the Sorgels recalled.

Mary Jane also continued to perform around the state and served as a judge for multiple pageants and competitions. She frequently appeared at halftime during the nationally televised Packers games and became a well-known personality around the state.

In 1959, Van Duyse trained in Clermont, Florida, to learn the art of water skiing while twirling the baton. She combined the two talents to appear in five travel films to promote Central Florida attractions. By then, she had already appeared in several radio and TV shows, including the Ed Sullivan Show and the Jack Eigen Show.

Van Duyse helped promote the Citrus Tower in Clermont, which opened in July 1956 to showcase the thriving citrus industry in the area. The tower provided a 360-degree panoramic observation deck to see approximately 35 miles in any direction.

That year, Mary Jane was also hired to help promote the movie "Big Circus" during a publicity tour in the Midwest. The movie starred Victor Mature, Red Buttons, and Rhonda Fleming, with a plot that revolved around a circus owner trying to keep his financially troubled circus afloat. The movie premiered in Wisconsin in connection with the Circus World Museum opening in Baraboo.

Mary Jane Van Duyse led a Mosinee caravan to the city's Athletic Park in July 1957, to help advertise Mosinee's centennial celebration.

Pictured above is one of Mary Jane's more notable cheer uniforms — a green and gold sequin unitard, paired with sparkly gold lace-up boots.

The Two Rivers Reporter said that Mary Jane got the movie promotion assignment when a hotel manager in New York City saw her and recommended her to Manny Goodman of Allied Artists. Van Duyse was in New York City with the Weyauwega High School Band for the Lions International Convention and performed with them at Wisconsin Night at Madison Square Garden.

She also joined the band prior to the New York trip to help raise money for the band's travel. The Weyauwega band was there to play for the inauguration of Clarence Sturm of Manawa as he became president of Lions International. Sturm is now memorialized through the organization's Birch-Sturm Fellowship, presented to Lions "who exemplify dedication and commitment" to the organization.

The Golden Era

In the late 1950s, Purdue's Adelaide Darling was firing up crowds and causing controversy as the college's chief majorette performed for football matchups around the country. Accused of "excessive wiggling" and making a "disgusting exhibition," Darling made headlines across the country as the school's "Golden Girl."

Similar to Darling, Green Bay's Mary Jane Van Duyse was young, blonde, and often seen in gold sequins.

"After I did a solo routine at a Packers-Bears game at Wrigley Field, a sports writer from the Chicago Tribune called me the Green Bay Packers Golden Girl because I had on a gold-sequined outfit," Van Duyse-Sorgel told Voyageur magazine in 2004. "Then, in Green Bay, the nickname caught on."

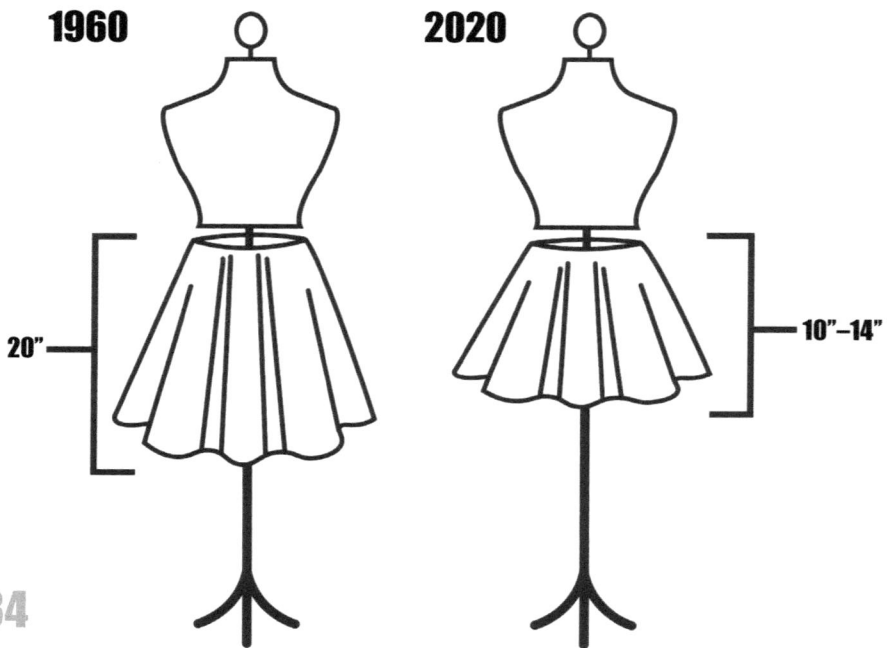

That Wrigley Field game — held September 27, 1959 — was also Packers Head Coach Vince Lombardi's first game.

"When Lombardi arrived in Green Bay in 1959, the Packers were coming off their worst season ever, a 1-10-1 finish, and hadn't had a winning record in 11 years. His first year, the Packers finished 7-5, and he was named NFL Coach of the Year," Packers Historian Cliff Christl stated.

"When Coach Lombardi came to town, he asked me if I'd form a group of cheerleaders. So we had an audition," Van Duyse-Sorgel recalled to the Door County Advocate in 2007. "When we started out, we had 16 girls from Sturgeon Bay and four from Green Bay. I always had rehearsals on Michigan Street in front of our house."

Their first full season on the field was in 1961, and every year after that, Van Duyse held tryouts before the Packers even started training camp.

"Most of our girls had been taking dancing and baton lessons," Mary Jane told Press-Gazette Staff Writer Judy St. John in 1966.

Vince Lombardi's wife, Marie, designed the uniforms in green, gold, and white, with modest skirts included in the uniform, per Vince's request.

The 20-person squad was augmented by four extras, should anyone be unable to perform. Most of the squad was of high school age.

"We practice our popular dance routines twice a week — once in Green Bay and once in Sturgeon Bay," Van Duyse explained. The girls were also subject to fines if they missed a session.

In 1966, Mary Jane opened a dance and baton studio in Green Bay, where she taught tap, acrobatics, ballet, modern jazz, and modeling. Local ads referred to it as "Golden Girl Studio."

Everyone's a Star

Around the time that Mary Jane opened her dance and baton studio in Green Bay, Carla Vandertie Coffey was just hitting the field as a Golden Girl. Carla, however, had been twirling since the age of five and had a longtime relationship with Van Duyse.

"She certainly was a positive role model for me. The light in her eyes when she smiled was always there, and she always had a smile for everyone," Coffey recalled. "What really sticks out for me is when we traveled together, it was not the Golden Girls, but three of her baton twirling students — a girl named Cheryl, her niece Susan, and myself. We would go to twirling competitions all over the Midwest because we were her twirling pupils, along with dance and Golden Girl stuff.

"But we were pretty young. Sometimes our mothers drove us, and we would stay for the weekend, but often, Mary Jane just drove the three of us. She would take responsibility to get us into our competitions fully costumed, made up, and warmed up for all of our events. We'd stay in a hotel and had an absolutely grand time.

"It seemed like it was during those times that I learned so much from her; she was always gracious, compassionate, patient with us, and she always made an impression on my life. But I think those more private times with her had the most impact. We learned a lot of life lessons just going to fancy restaurants and hotels, meeting people, and learning how to be gracious among people. You know, I was a farm girl from Brussels; these were all very exciting opportunities for me, and some that certainly my peers were not able to enjoy.

Mary Jane Van Duyse performs with her six-year-old niece, Susie Van Duyse, in the 1960s.

"Every year, we would have a recital and all of her students were featured in some way or another with their dancing, primarily. But then, of course, twirlers and soloists were in the recitals, and she wanted to make sure everybody would be a star on stage."

Carla would later take the field, serving as one of four accomplished baton twirlers stationed at each corner, where she said she was made to look "as teenage as possible." She performed as a Golden Girl from 1966 to 1972, ending her time on the field when she got married.

Passing the Baton

In July 1966, Van Duyse announced her retirement as the Packers drum majorette.

"I guess I'm the only girl in history who has been with a pro football team this long," she told the Press-Gazette's Lee Remmel. "I actually performed at one game in 1949 at the old City Stadium. That's when Curly Lambeau was coach and I was still in grade school."

Van Duyse turned her baton over to LeAnn Christiansen of Waukesha in September, literally tossing the baton to Christiansen in front of the Packers bench — which was reportedly fumbled. However, Van Duyse continued to work with the Packers organization as director of the Golden Girls.

"From 1951 through the 1972 season, for 22 years, Mary Jane never missed a game, nor did she ever miss a practice session," Jack Pearson wrote in 50PLUS in 2013.

"The girls were never paid anything," Mary Jane recalled to Pearson, "except for the games in Milwaukee and Chicago where they gave us an envelope with $3 in it to cover food or drink." The Golden Girls also paid for their pom-poms and uniforms.

During her time with the Packers, Van Duyse had become acquainted with former Packers Head Coach Curly Lambeau. However, according to Pearson, they had not officially met until Mary Jane's brother, Fritz, introduced them.

"I knew there was a big age difference between us," Mary Jane told Pearson, "I was about 24, and he was nearly 60, but right from the beginning, there was a spark, something there. He was so handsome, so intelligent, and so full of fun. I don't know how it happened, but we fell in love."

Mary Jane on the field in her "Golden Girl" uniform.

Van Duyse told Pearson that the two talked about marriage, but because she was Catholic and Curly had been married and divorced three times, her faith came between their vows. Their relationship would come to a tragic end when Lambeau had a fatal heart attack while pushing a lawn mower on the front lawn at Van Duyse's parents' home in Sturgeon Bay.

However, six months later, Van Duyse met William Sorgel, a management consultant and former president of Sorgel Electric Company. In June 1972, Mary Jane married Sorgel, and the couple began to split time between Key Biscayne, Florida, and Ephraim, Wisconsin.

Mary Jane left the Packers cheerleading group in the hands of Bernie Matzke, and they became known as the "Packerettes."

Mary Jane and Curly's relationship came to a tragic end when Lambeau had a fatal heart attack while pushing a lawn mower on the front lawn at Van Duyse's parents' home in Sturgeon Bay, pictured in 2025.

1919 – Inception of the Green Bay Packers.

October 23, 1928 – Press-Gazette releases a story on the Lumberjack Band claiming a world record for continuous playing without stopping for any reason.

1930 – Erich Karll copyrights and publishes the song "Go! You Packers Go!"

September 17, 1939 – The Lumberjack Band makes its first appearance rebooted as a "swing band", dressing in bright, colorful uniforms.

1940 – The Lumberjack Band Business Manager Wilner Burke is named band director.

1950 – Green Bay Packers are admitted into the National Football League.

1951 – Mary Jane Van Duyse becomes a Packer drum majorette.

1954 – Mary Jane wins the National Class A Baton Twirling Championship.

January 1955 – Mary Jane retires from competition but continues to be a majorette for the Lumberjack Band as well as teaching dance.

December 31, 1967 – The Ice Bowl game at Lambeau Field gives the Packers' home field its nickname "Frozen Tundra."

1920 1925 1930 1935 1940 1945 1950 1955 1960 1965

November 27, 1921 – The Lumberjack Band makes its first appearance cheering on the Packers against the Staleys in Chicago, Illinois.

1950 – Bernie Matzke creates and leads the Packerettes.

September 27, 1959 – Packers Head Coach Vince Lombardi coaches his first ever game at Wrigley Field against the Bears.

December 31, 1961 – Mary Jane starts the Golden Girls, and they have their first official performance at the NFL Championship game against the New York Giants.

1966 – Mary Jane opens a dance and baton studio in Green Bay and retires from Packers drum majorettes.

1972 – Mary Jane marries William Sorgel.

1988 – The Packers cheerleaders, now known as the "Sideliners" and led by Shirley Van, officially comes to an end.

1999 – The Packer Band (formerly the Lumberjack Band) is removed from the sidelines and takes its act to the tailgaters outside Lambeau Field before the game.

July 2, 2006 – Mary Jane's husband William Sorgel passes away.

1975 1980 1985 1990 1995 2000 2005 2010 2015 2020

1985 – Mary Jane and her Yorkie, Muffy, make their first appearance on "Stupid Pet Tricks" on the Letterman show.

September 2019 – The Door County Historical Museum opens a display to commemorate 100 years of Packers.

July 30, 2022 – Mary Jane Van Duyse-Sorgel passes away.

The Show Goes On

Mary Jane was set to headline the Miami Fourth of July Parade in 1973.

"Billed as 'The Golden Girl of the Green Bay Packers,' Mary Jane was to lead the Fourth of July parade, twirling a baton," The Miami News stated. "But the band she was to join didn't show." Always one to make sure that the "show goes on," Mary Jane joined the parade instead of leading it.

Mary Jane continued to teach young students, and in 1974, two of her Sturgeon Bay students — Jeff and Jody Zahn — took international honors at the world championships in baton twirling held in South Bend, Indiana.

She continued to make appearances in Wisconsin and Florida throughout the next decade. In 1984, she made newspapers all across the country when she was featured in a story about "Late Night with David Letterman" and its staff member, Sue Hall, who was in charge of finding talent for "Stupid Pet Tricks."

"Stupid Pet Tricks" was a staple of the David Letterman show from 1982 to 2015, featuring animals performing unusual, and sometimes silly, tricks. A reimagined version of the iconic segment was brought back on TBS in 2024, hosted by Sarah Silverman. In 1984, Sorgel sent in a videotape of her in a red-sequined drum majorette costume and high heel boots.

"As an off-camera accompanist strummed a guitar, likely her husband, and dolefully sang 'How Much is That Doggie in the Window?' Sorgel twirled a baton while balancing a Yorkie on her head. It was difficult to tell where the teased hairdo ended and the fluffy dog began," the Orlando Sentinel stated.

Mary Jane and her Yorkie, Muffy, appeared on Late Night with David Letterman twice — once in 1985, pictured, and again in 1986. Here, Mary Jane is pictured with her husband, Bill.

Hall called Mary Jane "a sure thing" for the show. She went on to make an appearance not once, but twice, on the Letterman show.

Mary Jane was featured on several TV shows with her Yorkies.

Following her original appearance, Van Duyse-Sorgel was brought back on the show in February 1986.

After the show's fourth anniversary, Letterman and crew brought a 747 to Florida, where three in-flight "Stupid Pet Tricks" were filmed — including Mary Jane and her dog, Muffy. Mary Jane and Muffy were highlighted on the show as the best "Stupid Pet Trick of 1985."

Van Duyse-Sorgel also appeared on the "Sally Jessie Raphael Show" and landed in the Guinness Book of World Records for the routine she and Muffy performed while traveling in the 747 for Letterman.

A Great Love Story

Mary Jane and Bill Sorgel's relationship spanned 34 years, which she referred to as "a great love story." The pair enjoyed being active and shared a love of scuba diving, fishing, cross-country skiing, performing for friends, traveling, and Yorkies.

However, Mary Jane still found time for her second love — the Green Bay Packers — joining her former Golden Girls to provide entertainment throughout the Northeast Wisconsin community. She also contributed a significant amount of charity in the communities she called home.

"Although Mary Jane spent part of each year in Florida, her heart was always in Sturgeon Bay. She was often a guest presenter for social and civic organizations, and she loved staying involved with the people and activities in Sturgeon Bay," said former Golden Girl Carla Coffey.

Mary Jane and Golden Girl Carla Coffey on the field.

"Mary Jane invited her niece, Susan Heimbecher, and me to join her at the Adult and Disability Resource Center (ADRC) for an appearance one time. We shared our memories of our Packer days, and yes, we performed routine number six — pom-poms and all. The audience loved it and asked so many questions."

"I remember Mary Jane doing some cheers at the Senior Center and at Pine Crest Assisted Living, complete with glitzy Packer attire," added Golden Girl Mary Wulf. "She would ask a few of us Golden Girls living in Sturgeon Bay to join her; usually, it was during the football season. She organized many gatherings with alumni over the years, including joining a parade across the new Bayview Bridge in Sturgeon Bay."

Mary Jane participated in telethons in Michigan and Wisconsin, and brought back the Golden Girls for the "Green and Gold Galas."

In July 2006, her husband Bill passed away. The following year, Mary Jane was presented with the Wisconsin Dance Council's Lifetime Achievement Award.

She was also highlighted in the "Legends on Parade," which commemorated the 50th anniversary of Lambeau Field, along with Bart Starr, Paul Hornung, Willie Davis, Jerry Kramer, and other Packers greats.

She later found companionship with an old childhood friend, Jack Champeau. She lost Champeau in 2018. Through all of the love and loss, one passion remained. "She just had so much zest for life and enjoyed her Packer memories until the day she died," Wulf added.

Mary Jane, standing in white, pictured with Bob Harlan and a group of Golden Girls at a Packers Hall of Fame event.

A Lasting Impression

Mary Jane Van Duyse-Sorgel passed away during the summer of 2022, leaving a long legacy that still reverberates inside the stadium walls of Lambeau Field.

"Coach Lombardi wanted to get the fans going. And then I decided we'd do 'Go, Pack, Go.' And to this day, I keep saying 'They're doing it again,'" Mary Jane told NFL Films in 2017.

"You know, I thought Mary Jane and the Lumberjack Band were wonderful," former Green Bay Packer Guard Jerry Kramer told the Milwaukee Journal-Sentinel. "She was attractive and enthusiastic. She really looked like she was having fun. She was a Packers celebrity — no question about it. She did a lot of telethons, parades, and dinners, and was very visible for the franchise throughout the year.

"You know, ball players and coaches don't last that long. She has to be one of the longest-serving personalities connected to the team."

The Door County Historical Museum hosts an exhibit dedicated to Van Duyse-Sorgel and the Golden Girls that's been on permanent display since September 2019. The exhibit, named "Mary Jane and the Golden Girls," features uniforms from 1959 to 1972.

Possibly the most indelible mark she left behind is the influence she had on her students, friends, and former Golden Girls. Michele Ozkan had a chance meeting with Van Duyse-Sorgel at a baton twirling camp in 1967. When Van Duyse-Sorgel offered her a spot on the Golden Girls, she jumped at it, though her experience was with twirling.

"I always looked longingly at the girls who were cheerleaders with the big fluffy pom-poms," Ozkan told reporter Anna Brugmann in 2016. Hearing the words pom-poms, Ozkan began traveling between Pottstown, Pennsylvania, and Van Duyse-Sorgel's home in Sturgeon Bay to cheer on "The Pack."

She later attended college in Wisconsin and continued to cheer. The team was just returning from a win in the NFL's first Super Bowl when Ozkan started.

"Had I realized what I was encountering ... I probably would have been frightened," Ozkan said. "But I just went in with a carefree heart, and I got to use those big pom-poms."

Ozkan credits Mary Jane for her greatest adventures, including the opportunity to take over her dance studio. There, Ozkan realized her passion for working with children. Mary Jane also provided something that she gave to a long line of young women in those days — confidence and the desire for perfection.

Mary Jane's Golden Girls line up to do a final cheer for her at her funeral.

"Meeting Mary Jane has been the single most important factor that has changed my life over and over again. I don't believe that it was a coincidence. I kind of believe it was meant to be."

—*Michele Ozkan*

The Golden Girls

by Tori Wittenbrock

The Women on the Sidelines

The Packers have one of the most storied histories of any football team in the NFL. Though the Golden Girls are an important part of that legacy, their stories of performing routines on Lambeau Field while donning their signature gold sparkle uniforms have often been buried deep in Wisconsin lore to be only vaguely remembered by those who had the pleasure of witnessing their routines in person.

Yet, in a time when society embodied a "woman-behind-the-man" mentality, the Golden Girls were truly breaking glass ceilings by putting young women on a stage — rather, a field — typically reserved for men.

Cheerleading history with the Packers runs much deeper than many avid football fans often realize. In the 31-year gap between the Green Bay Packers' inception in 1919 and their admission into the National Football League (NFL) in 1950, the startup team, led by Curly Lambeau, toyed with the idea of cheerleaders a few times.

In the 1930s, the Packers consisted primarily of Green Bay East and West High School graduates, and the team would often fill its sidelines with cheerleaders from the respective high schools.

However, as the sport of American football became more popularized, society began to experiment with the impact of cheerleading — not only for aesthetic or entertainment purposes — but for genuine boosts in morale and team spirit.

According to a 1937 Green Bay Press-Gazette article by sports editor John Walter, "Looking up in the realm of sports," Walter stated, "Green Bay as a community, at which this time of year presumably finds its greatest sports interest in the Packer football team, doesn't make enough use of the Packer pep song. While the use of cheerleaders, mascots and other synthetic spirit-awakeners at professional football games is hardly recommended, the fact remains that little details calculated to get football players and fans excited at important moments often play an important part in final scores."

Despite these early experiments, the concept of cheerleaders as a permanent addition to the Packers franchise didn't fully fall into place until the year 1950, when the Packerettes were instated under the leadership of Bernie Matzke. Matzke's squad of baton twirlers was instituted upon a suggestion from Lumberjack Band Director Wilner Burke. However, their role on the field for the next decade would stand mostly as a supplement to the band, and aligned more closely with baton twirling and marching than cheerleading.

A 1956 Press-Gazette article said that the Packerettes, consisting of 40 girls ages nine to 17, performed in their second nationally televised performance at halftime of a game. According to the article, "The Packerettes' program will include a precision kicking routine, their novelty act 'The Shake Routine' done to the tune of 'Alexander's Ragtime Band,' and a closing baton number."

At the time, little did Burke know that his influence on the world of NFL "cheerleading" was about to skyrocket. Burke's head drum majorette, 1954 baton twirling national champion, and Sturgeon Bay native, Mary Jane Van Duyse — later Van Duyse-Sorgel — was about to take a diligently selected group of young girls and transform them into one of the nation's first professional cheerleading squads in American football.

Outside of her love of baton twirling, Van Duyse-Sorgel had always been passionate about dance, opening several studios across Northeast Wisconsin to impart her knowledge and skill to the newest generation of dancers and performers.

It was primarily from these studios that the dedicated and glamorous crew — soon to be known as the Golden Girls — would be recruited.

By 1961, the women on the sidelines of Packers' home games had officially become known as the "Golden Girls." The name was a direct correlation to not only their gold sequin outfits, but also to their founder, Van Duyse-Sorgel, who became known as the Golden Girl after her baton performances. Van Duyse-Sorgel's nickname was, in turn, derivative of 1957-66 Packers Quarterback Paul Golden Boy" Hornung.

Judy St. John, staff writer for the Press-Gazette, stated in her 1966 article, "Golden Girls warming up for championship rally," that "Mary Jane organized the Golden Girls five years ago and, for a time, they performed on-field with their predecessors, the Packerettes. But soon that group disbanded and the 'Girls' have been dancing solo ever since."

The Golden Girls' first official game was the 1961 NFL Championship game — a 37-0 victory over the New York Giants played on December 31.

Public acceptance of the newest expansion of the Packers' franchise seemed overwhelmingly positive.

The Press-Gazette published a "Sneak Preview" of the Packers fans' hopes for the championship game and the Golden Girls inaugural performance, via the following poem — a December nod to "T'was the Night Before Christmas" by Carol Redaul — in the "People's Forum":

The Golden Girls squad poses for a photo during a home game at Lambeau Field, donning their traditional white sweaters emblazoned with a green 'P' letter, green and gold pleated skirts, white boots, and pom-poms.

49

"Twas the day before New Years and all through the stands

Not a person was silent (they were all Packer fans)

The players practiced along the field with care

With hopes that Paul Hornung soon would be there.

The viewers with blankets were warm as could be

While millions of others watched the game on TV.

Wilner in his suit and Vince in his coat

Were counting on victory, it was easy to note.

When out on the field there arose such a clatter

They sprang to their feet to see what was the matter

They looked up and down for the cause of the noise

They even questioned the Lumberjack Boys.

The roar of the crowd was deafening to hear

They wondered and worried about the cause of the cheer

When what to their wondering eyes should appear

But twenty Golden Girls and their glittering gear

With a charming teacher whose job was to train

They knew in a moment it was Mary Jane

More charming than experts her twirlers they came

And she whistled and twirled and taught each the same.

First Half of Game:

Now Max, now Bart, now Boyd, and now Paul

Now Jim; you guys get on the ball!

To the end of the field, to the goal you must run

Now dash away, dash away, and join in the fun.

They lined up for the start of the game right away

The kick was by Hornung, so what else need I say?

So over the goalpost, the football it flew

With it the hopes of a Giant victory, too.

Half-Time:

And then with the music as I watched through the half

Out came Mary Jane and all of her staff.

As I drew out my glasses to watch the girls twirl

I imagined the life of a Golden Girl

They were dressed all in gold from their heads to their feet

And their showmanship, not even experts could beat.

A green little tassel they had tied on their shoes

And I bet they could make the front page of the news.

Their eyes, how they twinkled, ever so gay

And I knew they were frozen on that cold winter day.

A twirl to the left, a kick to the right

And I knew that I'd dream of the Golden Girls that night.

Their bright batons they held tight in their hands

And their cute routine brought applause from the stands.

Mary Jane's smile was cheery for all

It made us Packer fans feel ten feet tall.

But the result of their practice showed at the end of their act

For they strut like champs, experts to be exact.

And holding their batons in the conventional way

They marched off the field on that victorious day.

Last Part of Game:

With two minutes left, it was 3 to 3

The suspense; the agony; it was killing me!

Packers had the ball, but their luck couldn't last

The seconds were running out all too fast.

Vince jumped from the bench; to his team gave a call

Down the field they thundered, holding onto that ball

And I heard him exclaim at the end of the game

A Championship, boys, to add to our fame!"

The Golden Girls pose for an on-field photo at Lambeau Field.

One of Van Duyse-Sorgel's original dance students and Golden Girls recruits, Sandy Borkovetz, said that Van Duyse-Sorgel's influence on her life, as well as her experiences with the Golden Girls, changed the course of her life.

"I moved to Sturgeon Bay in 1969. If it hadn't been for Annie Maedke, I never would have known because I didn't grow up cheerleading in high school, so it was all new to me. I had to learn how to twirl and do the dances," said Borkovetz.

Fellow Golden Girl cheerleader Anne Maedke said that the process of becoming an NFL cheerleader at the time was very different from what we see now, though the atmosphere was equally as competitive.

"In my experience, Mary Jane had an eye for picking out what type of talent or potential someone had. If she saw someone at a dance recital or twirling contest, she would nurture them and invite them to become a student," said Maedke. "For a dollar a session, my mother had paid for me to do acrobatics and tap dancing when I was about eight or nine. Throughout the years, Mary Jane had invited me to practices with her cheerleading squad, not mentioning any of the details."

Carla Coffey, who cheered with the Golden Girls from 1966 to the end of the 1972 season when Van Duyse-Sorgel retired, said that her life, too, was completely changed by the opportunity to cheer on Lambeau Field.

"I was a farm girl from Brussels. These were all very exciting opportunities for me," said Coffey.

St. John added, "The peppy entertainers begin preparing for football season in early summer, about the time the Packers come to training camp. Before that, Miss Mary Jane Van Duyse of Sturgeon Bay, director of the group, holds tryouts for aspiring Golden Girls."

Becoming a part of the select group often required taking dance lessons with Van Duyse-Sorgel for an extensive amount of time, as well as acquiring a personal invitation to the tryout.

Maedke noted that Van Duyse-Sorgel was the sole reason that the Packers were able to find their way to the forefront of NFL cheerleading.

"From that nurturing of us, came her desire to put together the cheerleading squad that was far and beyond what anybody in this territory ever saw, which became the Golden Girls," said Maedke.

Though Borkovetz and Maedke said that they now realize what they were a part of was a significant step for women — to have a platform in the NFL — at the time, they underestimated the value of their opportunity.

"I was about 13 when she called one morning and said, 'Annie, I'd like to see if you're interested in going to the Packers game. Some of the regulars are saying it's too cold,'" said Maedke.

Little did Maedke know what she was agreeing to with her first game on the field, being the notorious December 31, 1967, Ice Bowl game at Lambeau Field. Conditions were brutal with a reported temperature of -13 degrees and a windchill of -48 degrees. The matchup gave the Packers' home field its nickname of the Frozen Tundra.

"Her call was like three hours before game time. We were on our way to what would be known as the most outstanding, auspicious game of the century. It was quite a baptism by fire," said Maedke.

The Ice Bowl arguably proved the Golden Girls among the braver and more dedicated people in attendance at the game.

A January 2, 1968, Press-Gazette article entitled, "Field Electric Blanket Just Couldn't Cope with the Cold," by sports writer Jim Zima, stated, "Eight Hunter space heaters... were used on the field. Three were put at each bench...

The Green Bay Packers introduced the "Sideliners" from 1977-1986 after the Golden Girls enjoyed a brief return to their original "Packerettes" name from 1973-1977.

The remaining two were placed near the Packer band in an effort to keep the bandsmen and the Golden Girls warm. Despite the cold, the Packers Golden Girls were dressed in their tights and mini skirts to perform for the fans. Prior to the game, the girls came out in a formation with letter cards hanging on them proclaiming, 'Happy New Year From Green Bay.'"

Coffey recalled her own experience with Van Duyse-Sorgel's 'the show must go on' attitude.

"When I was twirling, we would take our sweater and skirt off and wear our gold sequin costume to twirl in the corners. I put my baton under my arm, and it was so cold that I remember letting out an 'Ahhh!' and I was just glad nobody on the field could hear that, but it was so cold!" said Coffey.

The Golden Girls became known as trailblazers in the professional cheerleading community, but in the 1960s and early 1970s, their platform was not quite the same as today.

"We didn't have to pay anything. We got our uniforms, but we had to pay for our own pom-poms. A while down the road, we were given a set of pom-poms, but boy, we had to be responsible with those," said Maedke. "It was fun and it was good exposure to the wild world of professional football, and it was a segway into avenues that we never would have dreamed of being exposed to."

In a nod to her own memory of the significance of the Golden Girls' pom-poms, Coffey said, "I had been offered money for my pom-poms numerous times while walking off the field, but Mary Jane would not have been happy. We all knew that, so we never sold our pom-poms. We went through a lot of pom-poms, though, because they were paper. Girls don't dance with paper pom-poms anymore, but I still have my pair."

According to Borkovetz, cheering for the Packers was one of the best experiences of her life, but the ladies on the field were also held to high standards in their line of work.

"Mary Jane was very much after a June Taylor, Rockettes-type look with the high kicks, especially at the half-time shows. You really had to be doing your stretching exercises in order to have your toe above your forehead. She was very particular about that and the timing of it so that we were all in unison," said Borkovetz.

Van Duyse-Sorgel's vision for the Golden Girls was nothing short of perfect, making it well-known that she had the highest of standards and expectations for her performers. St. John also noted that Van Duyse-Sorgel relayed to her that if any girls were to miss one of their practices in Sturgeon Bay or in Green Bay, they would be subject to a fine.

"We would gather mostly on the sidewalk at 552 Michigan St. (Sturgeon Bay). That was her family home. The sidewalk was a little bumpy, so she would make sure we stayed off the cracks so we wouldn't fall. The sidewalk led to just a little hill, and she would stand at the top of the hill and watch us, and we had to smile while we practiced," recalled Coffey. "The practices were sometimes hot. It was very hot during the summer, but we would get a water break. Granny Mae, her mother, would come out and watch us. She would love the ones who were smiling and really putting their effort into practicing hard and making a lot of movement."

Borkovetz said the professionalism that was instilled in her from a young age by Van Duyse-Sorgel is something that has stuck with her, decades after she was last on the field.

"We were also under 'no dating' the players rules. That was part of it as well, so as much as people would think we got to know the players, we've known them better after being off the field because we would see them at signings and events," said Borkovetz.

While Borkovetz and Maedke said that it was an honor to be on the field with the players at such a great era in football, Van Duyse-Sorgel ensured that their role would pair the glamour with a fair amount of dedication and hard work.

Mary Jane poses with a car featuring her name before a parade.

The First to Do It

Though they were trailblazers in the NFL cheerleading industry, the Golden Girls didn't know exactly what they were a part of when it all began.

"I never mentioned it. I never spoke about it as being a big deal. It was just another thing to do. Mary Jane would say, 'Okay, we are going to have another parade in this place.' We would drive across the state sometimes to Milwaukee or Chicago for fundraisers, and we didn't really think of it as a big deal," said Maedke.

With the expansion of NFL cheer over the years, the Golden Girls said that it has really helped them to realize the importance of their role as women on the field at that time.

"The first time the lightbulb went off was when the exposure of some of the other professional teams started popping up with really extraordinary and elaborate cheerleaders for other teams. We were the first ones in the league to have that opportunity, with routines and field entertainment. While the band played, there was something for the people in the stands to watch. It was designed as entertainment to fill in the blanks," said Maedke.

NFL cheerleading gained significant popularity in the 1970s; it was during this time that the Dallas Cowboys Cheerleaders began to gain recognition.

However, Golden Girl Sandy Borkovetz said that the ladies were just proud to be on the field and never received any financial reimbursement for their time.

"The only time we ever received money was when we took the bus with the band to the stadium in Milwaukee. On the way home, we'd pull over and stop at the Big Boy on Port Washington Road on the east side of Milwaukee. Wilner Burke would stand in front of the steps and as we each got off, he'd hand us a white envelope — inside were three single dollar bills so we could buy a Big Boy and a soda. That was our big treat," said Borkovetz.

According to Borkovetz, the experience in itself and the appreciation and support from the Packers fan base was rewarding enough.

"Really, it was the fans who gave us the motivation, and we could see by their appreciation that it was growing and catching on, and each year we were back on the field. You could see the fans were taking a liking to us. Even to this day, a few years back, you would go anywhere in Green Bay with Mary Jane, and people would stop and want to take your picture. They'd recognize her," said Borkovetz.

Borkovetz and Maedke said that the Golden Girls would have never existed had it not been for Mary Jane Van Duyse-Sorgel and Vince Lombardi.

"From what I know, Lombardi wanted a group of girls on the field and approached her because she appeared at Wrigley Field and there was an incident with her dropping

In addition to twirling and performing dance routines, the cheerleaders were often tasked with crowd work, holding up signs and cue cards to involve the people in the stands.

a baton and the Chicago newspapers referred to her as the "Golden Girl" so I think it was from there that Lombardi knew she'd be the person to do it," said Borkovetz.

Borkovetz's story is corroborated by the 1973 Press-Gazette article, "Golden Girl still glitters," in which staff writer Lois Kerin stated, "It wasn't 'dem golden slippers' of lyrical fame, but golden boots that gave the former Mary Jane Van Duyse the name by which Green Bay Packer fans were to recognize her for 21 years. Viewing her performance in the Windy City in 1951, a Chicago Tribune sportswriter referred to her as 'Green Bay's Golden Girl.'"

As the group continued to establish themselves as an integral part of the Green Bay Packers franchise, public support of the gameday experience continued to grow.

A 1965 "Packer Cheer Girls" photo in the Press-Gazette referred to the Golden Girls as a group of young ladies who, "add considerable color to all Packer games in Green Bay and Milwaukee," with Van Duyse-Sorgel and her niece Susie among them.

According to the Golden Girls, there was a lot of diligent planning and thought that went into each performance.

"Mr. Lombardi would talk to her about putting together some kind of two-minute warning show better than high school. Colleges had some cheerleaders, but he had some kind of dance routine in mind, rather than vocal cheers. The television and filming of these games wasn't such a big deal. People didn't really have TVs until the late 60s because they were still a luxury item," said Maedke.

Each Golden Girl had their own specific role on the field, which was to be taken seriously in preparation and performance.

"On the field at any one time, we had four squads of four, which meant that there were 16 of us in total. Each corner of the field had a group of four girls and then there were back-ups in case someone fell ill. They could move up through the ranks like I did by tolerating the cold," said Maedke. "There were broken legs, sprained ankles, and Mary Jane had to be ready. This was serious business. This wasn't just a little backyard barbecue entertainment. This was professional football, and she took it very seriously and she delivered," said Maedke.

Because the Golden Girls were among the first to set the standard for NFL Cheer, expectations from the franchise, as well as the fans, were high.

"We were very well-respected and enjoyed. Mary Jane, with us, was the one who started the 'Go Pack! Go!' chant. That's how we would get the crowd going. One girl held a sign that said 'Go', and I held the one that said 'Pack!', and we would just get the crowd roused by saying 'Go Pack! Go!' and obviously it stuck for all these years. We also yelled things like 'De-fence!' and tried to engage the crowd as much as possible," recalled Coffey.

Several generations of Packers fans have heard the very same chants continue to echo through Lambeau Field on imperative downs.

Mary Jane Van Duyse and Vince Lombardi walk the sidelines together in 1961.

A Lasting Experience

Despite their hard work on the field to ensure they knew their routines, the Golden Girls had high expectations for their public relations abilities as well.

"We started doing so many engagements, speaking-wise, and were invited to come here and go there, so we actually made a photo board so that the team could travel with us," said Borkovetz.

Even though the Golden Girls were often viewed as supplementary to the football team, the cheerleaders were an integral part of many of their banquets and events. Borkovetz said that the Packers coaching staff and administration were always very supportive of their efforts.

One time at an event, Borkovetz said that the cheerleaders even received a special callout.

"When (Holmgren) arrived, we were all sitting at the Golden Girls table and Mary Jane said, 'Get up there — you're doing the interviews.' We didn't know anything — all we knew was that he was Mike Holmgren," said Borkovetz. "I got up there and gave a brief history of the Golden Girls, and we had already been off the field for several years. I introduced him — which was a great thrill — but no matter what the situation was, the fans really cheered us on."

Borkovetz said that Holmgren even gave his verbal approval of the girls' support. "He came on the mic and said, 'If winning means bringing the cheerleaders back...' and then he yelled real loud, 'They're back!'"

Because of the support they had at each of their public outings, Borkovetz said that the Golden Girls always felt a welcomed part of the Packers organization.

"Bob Harlan was a huge supporter of us. Really, all the coaches, no matter where we were. After that introduction with Mike Holmgren, no matter what event or what gala we were at, I didn't even have to walk up to him. He came up to me and would talk," said Borkovetz. According to Borkovetz, the strict rules preventing fraternizing with coaches and players only limited them while they were active cheerleaders, but years after they had left the field, reconnecting with players and coaches was common.

"The key to talking to all the players and coaches was that they never wanted to talk about football. They wanted to talk about their family and where they lived. That's how Mike (Holmgren) was. He was very personable and a very easy guy to get along with. So was Bob Harlan," said Borkovetz.

Borkovetz also said that one of her experiences as a cheerleader gave her a glimpse of fame without realizing it.

"On the day Ray Nitchke was retiring, we were going through the tunnel and I was standing right behind him. I didn't realize that the picture would become one of his more famous shots. One time, I went to see Ray at an autograph signing at a K-Mart or something, and I walked up to the table. I didn't have anything for him to sign, but I said 'Hey, Ray. That's me in that picture.' He threw up his hands and said, 'Get up here and start signing!'" said Borkovetz.

Though the Golden Girls haven't performed on Lambeau Field in several decades, Borkovetz said that the experiences she gained from cheering on the Green Bay Packers were life-changing.

According to Coffey, having a run-in years later with a Packers player seemed inevitable for the Golden Girls.

"I do remember Boyd Dowler running me over once on the sidelines, and he looked down at me, and I remember thinking, 'Oh my gosh, he has no teeth.' He just had on a mouth guard, but at the time, I didn't know that," said Coffey.

The Packers Cheerleaders keep the crowd engaged under the lights at Lambeau Field.

"A couple of years ago, at a Bart Starr event at Rawhide, my husband was a volunteer at Rawhide, and we were invited to have a couple of seats at this event. It was part of the organization that Bart Starr was very impactful in founding. Boyd Dowler was there honoring Bart Starr, and I told him what had happened. He just laughed and said 'I don't remember looking you over, but I guess you are no worse for the wear.'"

Borkovetz, Maedke, and Coffey all agreed that the relationships they made through the Green Bay Packers community with each other and others have had a major impact on their lives.

"We could all get together in the same room and rekindle our relationships and our friendships on a moment's notice. At Mary Jane's funeral a couple of years ago, some of us went to the Sturgeon Bay Yacht Club afterwards, and you could have thought we were all still a part of the group the way we carried on with family stories and memories," said Coffey.

An Evolving Presence

The Golden Girls were no doubt part of a special and iconic time in Green Bay Packers history, incomparable to the NFL cheer industry today.

"We were never tuned into anything like 'Oh, how do I look? How's my hair? Where's the camera?' It wasn't about us. It was always about the Packers," said Maedke.

Despite their humility on and off the field, the storied legacy of the original Packers cheerleaders brought the interest of the media and the local community.

Borkovetz said that she is able to recall when a Press-Gazette writer stated that his interview with Mary Jane Van Duyse-Sorgel was one of the best in his career.

"This particular writer said he waited 58 years to meet Mary Jane of the Golden Girls and then went on to do this whole article on her. It was neat to read this whole article from a fan's perspective — who happened to be a writer — on the Golden Girls," said Borkovetz.

In Lois Kerin's 1973 article, she also details the impact Van Duyse-Sorgel had on not only the Golden Girls but the Packers and the cheer industry as well.

She stated, "Mary Jane also twirled her way into the Green Bay Packer Hall of Fame, and is the only woman in the hall."

Van Duyse-Sorgel's iconography extends far beyond the decade that the Golden Girls graced the sidelines of Lambeau Field.

The Door County Historical Museum has a display case honoring Van Duyse-Sorgel and her legacy with the Golden Girls. The display features a variety of photos, memorabilia, and uniforms.

Kerin added, "Mary Jane literally 'grew up' with the Packer band. She made her initial appearances in the old City Stadium and was part of the contingency during the tenure of each coach."

Though the vision of Lombardi, Burke, and Van Duyse-Sorgel was not always as perfectly executed as they had hoped.

Kerin's interview with Mary Jane also brought to light some of the not-so-golden moments in the Golden Girls' time on the field.

"Twice on the field, Mary Jane goofed. 'Once, I wasn't paying attention and almost led the band right into the stands,' she laughed. 'Another time,' she continued, 'I was late with the whistle while the band was executing a counterpoint routine. Fortunately, they were so alert and so well-trained that they proceeded without delay,'" wrote Kerin.

Maedke also recalled one time that their routine went up in flames — literally. According to Maedke, having shorter, thinner hair was a recipe for disaster, and her ponytail catching fire from a stray flaming baton became a lesson for all the other girls on the field as well.

However, Coffey said her experiences as a twirler with the fire batons were among her personal favorites.

"I remember using fire batons for the bishop's charity game because that was always at night, and the fire batons would always capture the audience, except for my husband. He was sitting in the stands with his dad — he tells this story over and over now — and he would complain and say, 'Why do we have to watch these girls? I want to see football,' and then he ended up marrying one of them. Back then, he was all about football and the game," recalled Coffey.

In addition to being memorialized through the media, the Golden Girls' legacy has also been enshrined in some local museums, including the Green Bay Packers Hall of Fame and the Door County Historical Museum.

"We were put into the Sturgeon Bay museum. It's kind of humiliating to know that now you're not only in one museum, but two museums, but it is a nice display," said Borkovetz.

The museum display opened in September 2019 as a way to commemorate 100 years of the Packers.

Mary Jane Van Duyse-Sorgel passed away just a few years later, in July of 2022.

Not only is she credited with starting the Golden Girls, but Van Duyse-Sorgel is known as a pillar of what made the Golden Girls such a significant time in the history of the Packers and why they are so well-known today.

According to Borkovetz, the Golden Girls would be forgotten entirely if it weren't for Van Duyse-Sorgel's efforts to preserve photographs and memorabilia.

"Mary Jane's house was like a museum. She lived in Mequon for a while, and I lived in Brookfield. I knew what she was trying to do, so I was helping her archive some of the photos. Every time she sent me off with a batch of pictures, I made duplicate copies for myself. Now, in retrospect, I'm glad I did because if I hadn't, they probably wouldn't exist," said Borkovetz.

When the Golden Girls' time on the field came to an end in 1972, Borkovetz and Maedke said that it was hard to see their squad be replaced and eventually see the women on the sidelines disappear entirely.

"I remember Mary Jane asking me — because she was getting married — 'Carla, don't you want to take over teaching the Golden Girls?' Well, I was 18 and going off to college, and it was just such a foreign concept to me; it was hard to even think about that. But, don't think I haven't thought about that many times since, wondering what my life would have been if I had tried to do that," said Coffey.

When it came time for Van Duyse-Sorgel to move on with her life, the Packers, too, decided to move on from the Golden Girls.

Upon Mary Jane Van Duyse's engagement to Bill Sorgel, the 1950s Packerettes name was revived for a short time as the baton was passed back to Bernie Matzke. Yet, by the year 1977, the Packer Executive Committee arranged to have a new squad of cheerleaders brought in to follow the Golden Girls under the leadership of local dance teacher Shirley Van.

This "new and improved" squad, however, did not have quite the public reception the Packers had hoped for.

"Mary Jane got married, and she was between Milwaukee and Green Bay. While she was busy with her life, she was pushed out," said Maedke.

A 1978 Press-Gazette article, entitled "New Cheerleaders, Good-Bad News," detailed the ruffled feathers caused by the coup.

The article begins, "The Green Bay Packers call it 'a new entertainment image.' Bernie Matzke calls it 'a cold callous move,'" and then goes on to discuss the impending changes.

"The Packers have decided to go with the 'adult-look,' similar to that of the Dallas Cowboys and other National Football League teams."

Straying away from the midwestern modesty and wholesomeness so avidly embraced by the Cheesehead fanbase proved a dire misstep in the course of the Packers' cheerleading history.

Even Van Duyse-Sorgel recognized how far the changes had strayed from the original vision for the girls.

"We weren't the Dallas Cowgirls," said Van Duyse-Sorgel in a 2007 interview with the Green Bay Packers. "We were wholesome Midwest girls, because Vince Lombardi did not like real short skirts. He liked the girls to be more

The Packers' sidelines are filled with cheerleaders at a packed game at Lambeau Field.

modest, so that's the way we were."

According to the Press-Gazette article, Matzke stated her blatant disapproval of the transition with her words, "I just feel like Green Bay is losing a bit of its identity."

The final official group of girls on the field, led by Van, would come to be known as the Sideliners — a fitting name considering the Packers cheerleaders would be officially and indefinitely sidelined by the year 1988.

"Neither one of those other groups were on the field for very long. Mary Jane was never one to cast dispersions on anyone, no matter how much she was done dirty. All of a sudden, there was a competition about how these new girls were going to be in and the Golden Girls were going to be out," said Maedke.

After a long career on the field, Maedke said that she was

saddened to see the way it all came to an end.

"We were at one parade, and we were asked about these other dancers that were there. I remember saying that they were alright. It wasn't until later that I learned that they were basically auditioning to take over as the Packers cheerleaders. If I had known that, I probably would have made a different comment. I was only a freshman in college at the time," said Maedke.

According to Borkovetz, other acts found out quickly that what Van Duyse-Sorgel had put together was no easy feat.

"We were done in the '73 season, and then they had these other girls out there, but they didn't work out. Mary Jane was a one-off. She was a tough act to follow. She was a star and a true professional," said Borkovetz.

"Looking back at the whole picture at my age now, we didn't realize quite what we had with Mary Jane," added Maedke.

Van Duyse-Sorgel had a true passion for keeping her girls on the sidelines of the Green Bay Packers games and for keeping their legacy alive, long after she herself had passed.

"She and Bill Sorgel carved out a life. They had a house just down the road from my house in Sturgeon Bay. I remember how wonderful it was to go see her. She had a foyer full of Packers memorabilia. It was like going to mom's house and seeing your baby pictures up on the wall," said Maedke.

Original Golden Girl Mary Jane is shown above receiving an award from Packers Band Director Wilner Burke for her 21 years of service.

Once in a Lifetime

Having the chance to be a trailblazer in the professional cheerleading industry was a once-in-a-lifetime opportunity for some of the women in the Packers franchise — the Golden Girls.

"For me, it was the exposure of doing what we had been doing. I had been asked to speak — like at the State Capitol, or different events, and getting into sports marketing — so it was no big deal to get up in front of crowds of people who would come. I even did a cooking show with LeRoy Butler once. It prepared us to be able to not fear anything, especially when it came to speaking and being out in public. I'm always grateful for where the opportunity allowed me to go personally because I did a lot of publicity work afterwards," said Borkovetz.

Physically cheering on one of the greatest teams in NFL history is an unmatched memory, according to Borkovetz, but the secondary skills she learned while on Lambeau Field far surpassed dance routines and media training.

"At the same time I was doing this, I was working for the Door County Chamber of Commerce as a good-will ambassador for the county. Tourist buses would come into town, and I would hop on and narrate the whole history of Door County. That's probably something I wouldn't have been able to do prior to that," said Borkovetz. "It's interesting to see how much it changed all of our lives."

The opportunities that came as a secondary response to the experience of cheering for the Packers were life-changing for many of the girls, according to Maedke.

"A lot of us took paths we never would have gone down had it not been for the experience cheering on the Green Bay Packers field," said Maedke.

According to Maedke, many of the life lessons that were instilled in the Golden Girls were the result of the high expectations set for them by Van Duyse-Sorgel.

The classic Golden Girls uniforms, featuring a white sweater, a green 'P', and pleated green and gold skirts, were hand-picked by Vince Lombardi's wife, Marie.

"The thing that I want to make a bigger deal about is that we were brought up with a very wholesome attitude towards being everyone's equal. We weren't special, we were just part of the entertainment, and it was a really healthy environment," said Maedke. "I was so grateful to see the contrast of how human interaction in a positive way unfolds as opposed to how the world is today."

Maedke also recounted a special memory of being a young girl in a professional environment that was expected to embrace the rarity of her opportunity with poise.

"It was just the coolest thing to be able to stand there cheering them on as they were coming out of the tunnel," said Maedke. "Mary Jane would line us up outside the tunnel according to height. At 5'2", I was always at the end and would have to lean around to see them coming out. I remember thinking, 'I hope they don't mow me over.'"

Despite her age, Maedke said that she was never left without proper mentorship or guidance at the hands of Mary Jane.

"Some of us were so young. The girls who were older than us who were there and cheered and then moved on with their lives (and) left it to us. Mary Jane had a blend of the new girls with the old girls. We were never too green — she was really clever about how she did that so that it was always the same level of polished, of showmanship, the same accuracy and talent. It was nice that way," said Maedke.

Coffey said that in her experience, Van Duyse-Sorgel was looking to raise the girls on the field with the same care and high expectations as if they were her own.

"We were constantly reminded that we were professional and we had to act professional and be professional," said Coffey.

"This is what we were taught. It's what Mary Jane expected. If you had the respect for Mary Jane in the way she garnered that respect, you would just go out and do it on her behalf. Maybe I was just a rule follower or something, but I can't imagine not showing her the respect or professionalism that she expected. There were girls that would complain of the cold or skip out, or not come to every practice because they found something more important, but those girls were not treated as well as those of us that did. Sometimes they were held off from a game, but Mary Jane had her way of making sure we were all on board."

Though many of the girls were young, Van Duyse-Sorgel knew they were capable of taking on the job with grace and professionalism without being overwhelmed by the atmosphere of Lambeau Field.

"I looked at it like 'This is what we do.' It didn't take me long to grow up out there. I started young, but the years flew fast, and pretty soon I was one of the older girls. At that time, once you got out of high school, you moved on," said Coffey.

Despite the standards set by Van Duyse-Sorgel, Coffey added that the Golden Girls were, in turn, treated with the same level of respect by their leader.

"We were trained well. I was nervous to twirl a baton in front of all those people out there, and I had a solo performance once, and I dropped it — not proud of that — but Mary Jane would never scold. She would always say, 'Oh, you did great.'"

Borkovetz and Maedke said that reflecting on their experiences on the field has bred an interesting comparison to how different their role would have been in today's world.

"I went on to order pom-poms for Mary Jane's funeral and found they have a whole setup now for cheerleading. They didn't have that back then. You can say, 'I want that sweater with that skirt, and have 16 sets in the mail. Back in Mary Jane's day, she had to go through 32 magazines that were sent to her," said Maedke.

Nowadays, not only has the ease of access to cheer uniforms changed dramatically, but the once modest and respectable styles have changed as well.

"I've seen the pin-up look with the low-cut shirts and the midriffs showing. I can see the part that would sell, but it just kind of takes the imagination and the wholesomeness of the whole thing," said Maedke. "And there's nothing wrong with having some leggings on if it's 40 below."

Despite the "frozen tundra" conditions of Lambeau Field, Borkovetz explained that many of the Golden Girls had to experience the famed Ice Bowl according to strict uniform standards that didn't allow for modifications to their attire.

"You couldn't just get pantyhose anywhere that didn't have the dark lines around them. We're talking the late 60s when they would double-knit them from the thigh up so you could tell they were under the skirts," said Borkovetz.

Coffey said that their uniforms were designed by Lombardi's wife, Marie, and were not to be altered under any circumstances.

"Marie hand-picked out our uniforms — our skirts, scarves, and sweaters. I remember thinking, 'How are we going to dance in all of this stuff, but we made it work,'" said Coffey.

Though the NFL cheerleading culture has endured some major changes in its public perception over the years, Borkovetz and Maedke said that they will forever treasure the time in which they were able to occupy the sidelines at Lambeau Field.

"I can't say enough about the contrast I see when you ask the question of cheerleaders today. This is professional football. I know the goal is to get the attention of the fans, to interact, to market the pictures, and make a buck on it. If you're going to do that, well then, bring out some football cards or cheerleader cards and sell them for charity or something like that," said Maedke.

Coffey agreed, stating that she doesn't feel that many of the modern-day NFL Cheerleaders would do justice to the honor, respect, and professionalism that were paramount to the time in which Lombardi and Van Duyse-Sorgel first conceived the idea.

Since the dispersion of the Sideliners in 1986, the Packers' sidelines have remained relatively clear of cheerleaders, aside from the occasional guest appearance from local colleges, including St. Norbert College and the University of Wisconsin-Green Bay cheer squads.

"I have to say, the cheer teams that have been on the field, I'm a season ticket holder, I have not been proud of or proud to say I was one of them. Maybe I thought we were better than we were, but if a team were to go back out there, they would have to be very good. They would not have to be [scantily dressed], because that would not honor Vince Lombardi. He and Marie were very intent on us being modestly dressed," said Coffey.

"I still think a team could be put out there. Not scantily clad, but modest and on trend. I'd want them to be very good. I think it would be different. We were dancing to a live band and were never told what song would be next. Wilner Burke played what was appropriate at the time. He would pipe up, and Mary Jane would say, 'Number 6!' and we would line up and start Number 6. The other corners would see us start Number 6 and start up an eight-count later," added Coffey.

In the 2022 CNN article, "NFL cheer uniforms have been scrutinized since the 1970s, but critics might be missing the point," Jacqui Palumbo stated, "what cheerleaders represent — and what they wear — has long been a topic of public interest, raising questions about gender stereotyping and the fair treatment of cheer athletes. That's been the case since the Dallas Cowboys cheerleaders were broadcast in the 1970s on national television... This breakaway from the pleated skirts and modest tops seen throughout the 1960s ignited a fire.

"I think I would involve some kind of advertisement of the cheerleaders to advertise for a good cause. Yes, the Packers are a good cause, but couldn't you take that opportunity for this charitable endeavor and pass it on to honor the people like Curly Lambeau, Vince Lombardi, and Mary Jane Van Dueyse-Sorgel, and all the other older football players that made the game and put Green Bay on the map?"

Borkovetz said that her appreciation for the opportunity to be a Golden Girl has never faltered.

"We couldn't have had a better time than to be there with the likes of Willy Wood, Willy Davis, Henry Jordan, Ray Nitchzke, and Bart Starr. We wouldn't have had a better opportunity to cheer on a greater team in the whole history of the Packers," said Borkovetz.

The Golden Girls would perform their routines on cue when the Lumberjack Band would begin their next number. Pictured above, Lumberjack Band Director Wilner Burke stands for a picture on the sidelines with the Packers Cheer Squad.

68

Acknowledgements

Special thanks to Dr. Don Sipes, Sam Kluck, and Katie Foust of the Packers Hall of Fame Inc., Deb Anderson from the UW-Green Bay Archives, and Mary Jane Herber at the Brown County Library History Room. Your resourcefulness and knowledge were a large part of this book's development.

Many thanks to Pat Wood and Mike Hollihan for their support in moving forward with this project, and Dr. Rebecca Meacham, Alex Kunce, Jordan Sieracki, Ongnia Thao, Karly Wigand, Grace Zander, and Tori Urness at the UW-Green Bay Teaching Press for all of their hard work with this book.

Last, but not least, a big thank you to David & Sandy (Borkovetz) Stern for all of their assistance and networking along the way.

This would not have happened without you.

Kris Leonhardt

Inspired by the stories her grandmother told her while growing up, Kris Leonhardt has been chronicling North American history since she was a junior in high school. A student of Marquette University and the University of Wisconsin, as well as a US Army veteran, Leonhardt now works as a senior editor at Multi Media Channels (MMC). She is also a director with the "Pass it Forward" community journalism internship initiative, where she helps guide aspiring young writers and journalists.

Tori Wittenbrock

Tori Wittenbrock has had a passion for reading and writing from a very young age. After completing her English degree from the University of Wisconsin-Green Bay on a Division I soccer scholarship, she was able to merge her passion for athletics with academics by becoming a sports editor for the Green Bay Press Times through Multi Media Channels (MMC). Wittenbrock began her career as a journalist in 2023, covering local sports at the high school, collegiate, and professional levels through game coverage, feature stories, photography, radio, and podcasting.

Photo Credits

Cover:

The Golden Girls pose for an on-field photo at Lambeau Field. Green Bay Packers Hall of Fame Archives photo.

Title Page:

The Lumberjack Band performs at City Stadium in the early days of its formation. Germaine Pirlot family photo.

Table of Contents:

An early photo of the Lumberjack Band performing. Green Bay Packers Hall of Fame, Inc. photo

The Lumberjack Band:

Page 11: The Lumberjack Band performs at City Stadium in the early days of its formation. Germaine Pirlot family photo.

The Lumberjack Band Chapter Cover: An early photo of the Lumberjack Band performing. Green Bay Packers Hall of Fame, Inc. photo

Page 14: The Lumberjack Band poses with their musical instruments in 1923. Packers Hall of Fame photo.

Page 15: A 1929 ad invites fans to travel with the Lumberjack Band. Chicago & Northwestern Railway ad.

Page 16: An early photo of the Lumberjack Band performing. Green Bay Packers Hall of Fame photo.

Page 21: In 1940, Lumberjack Band Business Manager Wilner Burke was also named band director, a title he held until his resignation in the early 1980s. Packers Hall of Fame photo.

Page 22: In this undated photo, Wilner Burke is pictured at the far left standing. Harmann Studios photo.

Page 24: Carol Collard (second from left) is pictured with fellow Lumberjack Band majorettes Germaine Pirlot (left) and Gloria Birmingham (right) in 1944. Harmann Studios/Germaine Pirlot family photo.

Page 28: The Lumberjack Band on the field at City Stadium in an undated photo. Pirlot family photo.

Page 29: The Lumberjack Band performs at City Stadium in the early days of its formation. Germaine Pirlot family photo.

Mary Jane:

Chapter cover: The Golden Girls stand for a photo with their leader, head majorette, and champion baton twirler, Mary Jane Van Duyse.

Page 31: Mary Jane Van Duyse started her dance career at the Dorothy Leyse La Plant School of Dancing at the age of six. Three years later, she began twirling a baton and started wowing the crowds at regional festivals with her acrobatics and baton twirling skills. Van Duyse/Sorgel family photo.

Page 32: In this black-and-white photo, Mary Jane poses with her batons before a performance. David and Collette Sorgel photo.

Page 33: Mary Jane Van Duyse led a Mosinee caravan to the city's Athletic Park in July 1957 to help advertise Mosinee's centennial celebration. Wausau Daily Herald photo.

Page 34: Pictured above is one of Mary Jane's more famous cheer uniforms — a green and gold sequin unitard, paired with sparkly gold lace-up boots. Green Bay Packers Hall of Fame Archives/author photo

Page 36: Mary Jane Van Duyse performs with her six-year-old niece, Susie Van Duyse, in the 1960s. Van Duyse/Sorgel family photo.

Page 37: Mary Jane on the field in her "golden girl" uniform. Sandy Borkovetz photo.

Page 38: Mary Jane and Curly's relationship came to a tragic end when Lambeau had a fatal heart attack while pushing a lawn mower on the front lawn at Van Duyse's parents' home in Sturgeon Bay, pictured in 2025. Kris Leonhardt photo

Page 41: Mary Jane and her Yorkie, Muffy, appeared on Late Night with David Letterman twice — once in 1985 and again in 1986. Here, Mary Jane is pictured with her husband, Bill Sorgel. Sandy Borkovetz photo.

Page 42: Mary Jane was featured on several TV shows with her Yorkies. Sandy Borkovetz photo.

Page 43: Mary Jane and Golden Girl Carla Coffey on the field. Carla Coffey photo.

Page 44: Mary Jane, standing in white, pictured with Bob Harlan and a group of Golden Girls at a Packers Hall of Fame event. Sandy Borkovetz photo.

Page 45: Mary Jane's Golden Girls line up to do a final cheer for her at her funeral. Sandy Borkovetz photo.

Page 46: Mary Jane, still cheering at a Sturgeon Bay event in her later years. Sandy Borkovetz photo.

Page 55: Mary Jane poses with a car before a parade with a banner reading "Green Bay Packers' Golden Girl Mary Jane Van Duyse."

Timeline:

1921: The Lumberjack Band poses with their musical instruments in 1923. Packers Hall of Fame photo

1944: Carol Collard (second from left) is pictured with fellow Lumberjack Band majorettes Germaine Pirlot (left) and Gloria Birmingham (right) in 1944. Harmann Studios/Germaine Pirlot family

1975: Mary Jane Van Duyse marries Bill Sorgel. Here, they are pictured on Late Night with David Letterman. Sandy Borkovetz photo.

1985: Mary Jane and her Yorkie, Muffy, make their first appearance on "Stupid Pet Tricks" on Late Night with David Letterman. Sandy Borkovetz photo.

2019: The Door County Historical Museum opens a display to commemorate 100 years of the Packers. Author photo.

The Golden Girls:

Page 47: Mary Jane Van Duyse held "rehearsals" on Michigan Street in front of her family's house, pictured here. Mary Beth Drab/Harmann Studios photo.

Page 48: The Lumberjack Band performs at City Stadium in the early days of its formation. Germaine Pirlot family photo.

Page 50: The Golden Girls squad poses for a photo during a home game at Lambeau Field, donning their traditional white sweaters emblazoned with a green 'P' letter, green and gold pleated skirts, white boots, and pom-poms. Door County Historical Museum photo.

Page 53: The Golden Girls pose for an on-field photo at Lambeau Field. Green Bay Packers Hall of Fame Archives photo.

Page 55: The Green Bay Packers introduced the Sideliners from 1977-1986 after the Golden Girls enjoyed a brief return to their original "Packerettes" name from 1973-1977. Green Bay Packers Hall of Fame Archives photo.

Page 57: In addition to twirling and performing dance routines, the cheerleaders were often tasked with crowd work, holding up signs and cue cards to involve the people in the stands. Green Bay Packers Hall of Fame Archives photo.

Page 58: Mary Jane Van Duyse and Vince Lombardi walk the sidelines together in 1961. Green Bay Packers Hall of Fame Archive photo.

Page 60: The Packers Cheerleaders keep the crowd engaged under the lights at Lambeau Field. Green Bay Packers Hall of Fame Archives photo.

Page 61: The Door County Historical Museum has a display case honoring Van Duyse-Sorgel and her legacy with the Golden Girls. The display features a variety of photos, memorabilia, and uniforms. Author photo.

Page 63: The Packers' sidelines are filled with cheerleaders at a packed game at Lambeau Field. Green Bay Packers Hall of Fame Archives photo.

Page 64: Original Golden Girl, Mary Jane, is shown above receiving an award from Packers Band Director Wilner Burke for her 21 years of service. Door County Historical Museum photo.

Page 65: The classic Golden Girls uniforms, featuring a white sweater, a green 'P', and pleated green and gold skirts, were hand-picked by Marie Lombardi. Green Bay Packers Hall of Fame Archives photo.

Page 68: The Golden Girls would perform their routines on cue when the Lumberjack Band would begin their next number. Pictured above, Lumberjack Band Director Wilner Burke stands for a picture on the sidelines with the Packers Cheer Squad. Green Bay Packers Hall of Fame Archives photo.

Page 69-70: The Golden Girls pose for an on-field photo at Lambeau Field. Green Bay Packers Hall of Fame Archives photo.

www.ingramcontent.com/pod-product-compliance
Lightning Source LLC
Chambersburg PA
CBHW042056090526
44582CB00010B/165